FIVE-MINUTE

DEVOTIONS
for kids

Real Heroes Eat Pizza

TIM HANSEL

CHARIOT BOOKS
AN IMPRINT OF
CHARIOT VICTOR PUBLISHING

This book is dedicated to a young man
who gives real meaning to the word courage.

to
Kyle Woodard
who, in his ten years,
has displayed more courage per square inch
than anyone I've known.
I consider him a "best friend,"
(and not just in the Pacific Northwest),
a fellow writer, an inspiration,
and one of my
REAL heroes!

During one of his many stays at the Ronald McDonald House
in Seattle, he wrote me this poem:

TIM

Tim Tim I love you
when your pain is in gain.
Tim Tim I love you
when you're doing just fine
right down the line.
Tim Tim you're the best friend
anyone can find.
Tim Tim I love you
all the time.

and so Kyle, I decided to write this one to you in return:

Kyle Kyle I've known you
for a while.
Kyle Kyle I know you're in great pain
but you always smile.
In fact, the first time we met
we needed to stop for some toast,
And we ended up laughing all the way
to the Oregon coast.
I remember saying to myself that I'm
glad this relationship will last a whole lifetime.

Chariot Books™ is an imprint of Chariot Victor Publishing
Cook Communications Ministries, Colorado Springs, CO 80918
Cook Communications Ministries, Paris, Ontario
Kingsway Communications, Eastbourne, England

REAL HEROES EAT PIZZA
© 1995 by Tim Hansel

Previously published as Real Heroes Wear Jeans © 1989, and Real
Heroes Eat Hamburgers © 1989.

Cover design by Bill Paetzold.
Cover illustration by Gary Locke.
Interior illustrations by Joe Van Severen.

First printing revised edition, 1995
Printed in the United States of America
99 98 97 96   5 4 3 2

Library of Congress Cataloging-in-Publication Data
Hansel, Tim.
    [Real heroes eat hamburgers]
    Real heroes eat pizza / Tim Hansel.
        p. cm.
    Previously published separately: Real heroes eat hamburgers; Real
heroes wear jeans.
    ISBN 0-7814-0197-6
    1. Children–Prayer-books and devotions–English.   [1. Prayer
books and devotions.]   I. Hansel, Tim. Real heroes wear jeans.
II. Title.
BV4870.H25 1995
242'.62–dc20   94-35154
                                                              CIP
                                                              AC

TABLE OF
CONTENTS

TABLE OF
CONTENTS CONT.

STOP!
Read this first.

Have you ever wanted to be a hero. . .or at least brave enough to do what none of your friends dared to do? If you were a hero, people might use words like brave, gutsy, daring, courageous, and fearless, to describe you.

Some kids think heroes are only in comic books or maybe playing football for the 49ers, or making lots of money in a rock band. But real heroes are people like the friends you'll meet in this book. And when you've thought about it, I think you'll see how you can be a hero, too. That's why I've written this book. The world needs young people who know how to live like heroes. I hope you will be one of those young people who is willing to go on a real hero adventure.

Tim Hansel

HERO PRACTICE:

Some kids might say, "I don't know how I could ever be a hero." The section marked "Hero Practice" will help you find out what it feels like for you to be a *real* hero.

TAKE COURAGE:

God's Word is full of words of courage. When you see "Take Courage," a Bible verse will give you courage to be the hero God wants you to be.

PRAYER:

Sometimes it's difficult to pray. You want to say something to God, but don't know where to start. The prayers in this book will help you get started. Then you can add whatever you want to say to God.

ANSWER CHECK:

Make a check in the box when your prayer is answered. One of the best ways to build up your courage is to look back through the book and see how many prayers God has already answered.

Your words are important!

We've left you extra room throughout this book so you can write or draw your thoughts and ideas. Have fun!

About Tim Hansel . . .

Tim Hansel has done things most of us only dream about. He's sailed 25,000 miles on the Pacific Ocean in a forty-three-foot boat. He's climbed one of the highest mountains in the United States. He's worked with some of the toughest gangs in New York City, helping gang members get to know Jesus Christ.

After coaching high school soccer and college football, Tim started Summit Expedition, an organization that takes kids and adults on wilderness and mountain-climbing trips. One of the most exciting Summit programs is GO FOR IT, especially for handicapped people.

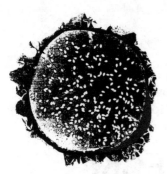

It's a Horse, Of Course

Bo Nixon and I had just arrived at the Young Life Colorado ranch with a load of kids from New York's inner city. One of the kids was Mike, whose gang name was "Hatchet Man." (Bo said, "because that's his favorite weapon.")

Mike pointed to an animal standing nearby and said, "Hey, what's that?"

"It's a horse," we told him, surprised that he didn't know.

"Naw, that's no horse," Mike said. "Horses ain't that big because I've seen 'em on TV and they're just little teeny things!"

Mike may not know much about horses, but that week at Young Life camp he became a real hero. That's because he had the courage to let Jesus Christ change his life from a tough New York City gang member to a person who decided to live for God.

HERO PRACTICE:

You may not live in a rough neighborhood, but it may still be hard for you to live for God where you are. Remember that God is with you as you think about living for Him this week.

TAKE COURAGE:

"The Lord is my light and my salvation—whom shall I fear? The Lord is the stronghold of my life—of whom shall I be afraid?" Psalm 27:1

 **PRAYER:**

Give me courage, Lord, to live for You this week.

 **ANSWER CHECK:**

Real heroes . . .
have courage to live for Christ.

The Heart of King Kong

I first met Sherry Leonard when she was a counselor at Young Life camp. And I wondered, how did this frail-looking girl who can't even walk get to be so happy? It was as though life just giggled and danced inside her. She had a heart as big as King Kong. Teenagers loved her because they could tell she loved them. And because she felt so good about herself, she made them feel good about themselves.

I found out that Sherry was nine when she began losing her muscle power. She had muscular dystrophy, an illness that paralyzes your muscles. For a few years she was discouraged because she couldn't get around like other people. She even asked God to help her die. Then she realized that God doesn't make mistakes.

Now she says, "Muscular dystrophy is my gift from God. It has made it easier to tell people about Jesus Christ." Sherry has learned to relax and leave her life in God's hands, because she knows that God can turn even muscular dystrophy into something good.

HERO PRACTICE:

If God can turn a handicap like Sherry's into something good, what problem of yours could you leave in God's hands?

TAKE COURAGE:

"Be delighted with the Lord. Then he will give you all your heart's desires. Commit everything you do to the Lord. Trust him to help you do it and he will."

Psalm 37:4, 5, TLB

PRAYER:

You know how big my problems seem to me, Lord. Thank You for being bigger than any of them. One problem that I would like to give to You is:

ANSWER CHECK:

Real heroes . . .
trust God with their problems.

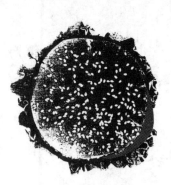

Blood Brothers

The first time I ate rattlesnake meat was with my friend Shelton Chow at his mom's restaurant. We had decided early on to be "blood brothers." So Shelton invited me to the special "family only" dinner at the restaurant, even though that made me the only person there who wasn't Chinese.

Shelton is on my list of real heroes because he was color-blind. Oh, there was nothing wrong with his eyes. He just refused to make a big deal about whether someone was white or black or brown or whatever. He even invited me to play in his all-Chinese basketball league. "This is my blood brother," he said when he introduced me to the group. So they let me play the whole season because of Shelton.

Shelton looked at people the way God does. What's really important isn't the color of our skin, but what we are like on the inside.

HERO PRACTICE:

Do you know some kids who look different than you do? Do you treat them the same as kids who are more like you? What would you need to do to be a hero to those kids who look different than you?

TAKE COURAGE:

". . .we are all the same. . .we are one in Christ Jesus." Galatians 3:28b, TLB

 **PRAYER:**

It's easy to forget, God, that You see us from the inside out. Help me to look at all the kids with eyes that are "color-blind."

ANSWER CHECK:

Real heroes...
are "color blind."

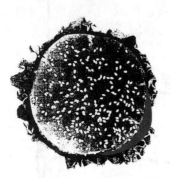

Oh, Wow!

I hated to think about climbing out of my warm and toasty sleeping bag even though it looked like the start of a beautiful day in the Sierra Mountains. Because I once broke my back in a mountain-climbing accident, it's always hard to move in the morning. So, I was kind of feeling sorry for myself that morning until I looked over and saw Tim Burton begin to struggle out of his sleeping bag.

Tim was a carpenter. One day he fell off a wooden construction platform and hit his head. Since that time he has not been able to walk, and has trouble moving and even talking. Now he was working as hard as he could to get out of that sleeping bag by himself. It took him half an hour! But he kept at it, and when he was finally out, he looked over at me and said in his stammering voice, "Ok-k-kay, Tim. I'm r-r-ready f-for a-a-a-anything!"

Later, as he struggled up the side of the mountain with the help of two instructors, he kept saying, "Oh, W-W-Wow!" He was so thankful to be making the climb, even though it was hard. We named the climb "Oh, Wow" after Tim Burton.

HERO PRACTICE:

Think of something that's hard for you to do. Then think about Tim Burton. How can you be a hero about difficult things?

TAKE COURAGE:

"And we pray this in order that you may live a life worthy of the Lord and may please him in every way. . .that you may have great endurance and patience." Colossians 1:10, 11

PRAYER:

Thank You for always being there to help when something seems too hard for me. I love You, Jesus.

ANSWER CHECK:

Real heroes...
never quit trying.

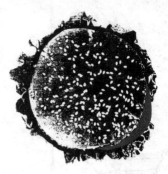

No Ordinary Dentist

Dr. Ken Campbell is no ordinary dentist. For one thing, he doesn't look ordinary. He has no eyebrows, and the skin around his eyes and mouth is pulled back tight. That's because he was burned very badly in a car crash several years ago. He and his girlfriend were waiting at a stop sign when their car was hit by a huge tanker truck. The car burst into flames. Ken's girlfriend was killed. The burns were so painful that Ken prayed that he would die. But God had other plans for him, and that's another reason Ken isn't an ordinary dentist.

Ken decided to not give up, and to let God help him get well. Now he often talks to people about Jesus while he fixes their teeth. He tells people that the reason he's alive is because of Jesus Christ. Sometimes he takes trips to Central America where he gives free dental help to people who couldn't get it otherwise.

HERO PRACTICE:

Maybe you think that if you were just a little older, or a little smarter, or if you knew the "right words," you could be a witness for Jesus. This week, remember how God helped Dr. Ken be a witness for Him, even when he thought his life was over, and then see how God can help you.

TAKE COURAGE:

"I tell you, whoever acknowledges me before men, the Son of Man will also acknowledge him before the angels of God."   Luke 12:8

PRAYER:

Sometimes I don't want to say anything about You, God, especially to kids who might laugh. Help me to be a witness for You even when I'm afraid.

ANSWER CHECK:

Real heroes...
live for Jesus right where they are.

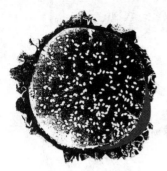

Rich Guy from Pittsburgh

Bill Milliken didn't know what he was getting into when he rode into a New York inner city ghetto ready to help. The kids he met there were tough and not sure they wanted any help from this Christian guy from Pittsburgh. Many of them were members of street gangs. They were used to living with fighting on the streets and at home.

Bill discovered one of the real meanings of *hero*—"a person who tries to help others no matter what happens." He kept on trying to learn how to do this, even though it was dangerous and discouraging. And many of the kids became Christians and changed their ways. One of them, Bo Nixon, president of the Young Pagans gang, now directs a ministry to street kids in New York City.

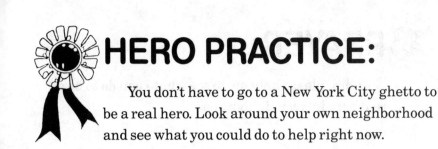

HERO PRACTICE:

You don't have to go to a New York City ghetto to be a real hero. Look around your own neighborhood and see what you could do to help right now.

TAKE COURAGE:

"The Lord himself goes before you and will be with you; he will never leave you nor forsake you. Do not be afraid; do not be discouraged."

Deuteronomy 31:8

PRAYER:

Lord, please help me to see what I can do to be a real hero in my neighborhood.

ANSWER CHECK:

Real heroes. . .
try to help others no
matter what happens.

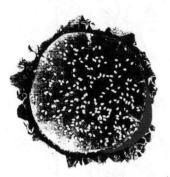

Try, Try Again

It takes a lot of courage to try something again when you think you've never been good at it. Pam had never liked school. She considered herself a poor student. When she managed to get through high school and a little bit of college she decided that was enough. It was just too hard.

But after she was married and her kids got older, she realized that she would have to go back to college to get the job she wanted. She was scared. But Pam knew it was worth trying again. Now she's glad she did because she was not only able to graduate from college, but then went on to get her master's degree to become a psychologist. This was something she had always wanted to do. Pam is a very important hero to me because she is my wife.

HERO PRACTICE:

Think of something you wish you didn't have to try to do again. It's just too hard. How can you have courage to try again?

TAKE COURAGE:

"I have set the Lord always before me. Because he is at my right hand, I will not be shaken."

Psalm 16:8

PRAYER:

Dear God, it's just too hard for me to _____

_____ .

Please give me the courage to try again. Thank You.

ANSWER CHECK: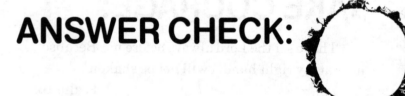

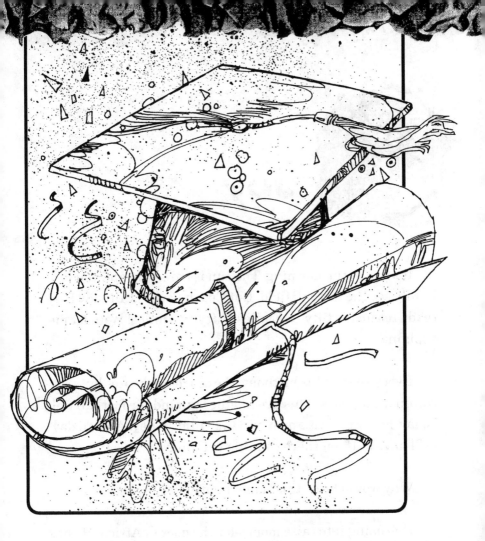

Real heroes...
keep going even when they feel like giving up.

Joy

It's five in the morning. The sun is barely up and you can hardly see the football field. But Coach Parks is already here ready to run his fifty-five miles. Fifty-five miles! Well, let me explain.

Every year on his birthday, the coach celebrates by running the years of his age in miles around the football field. Today, he's fifty-five, and it will take him all day. And all day he'll have kids out there running with him.

Why would he do this? I mean, fifty-five is old!

He's doing it to raise money for the poor in Africa. He has people pledge a certain amount per mile. You see, Coach Parks has discovered one of the meanings of joy: *J*esus first, *O*thers next, and then *Y*ourself. He knows he is happiest when he's doing something for other people.

HERO PRACTICE:

Think of a time when you did something for a person in your family or for a friend. How did you feel? You were probably feeling joy the way Coach Parks spells it—*J-O-Y.*

TAKE COURAGE:

"The joy of the Lord is your strength."

Nehemiah 8:10

 **PRAYER:**

Feeling joy is great, Lord. I want to remember to live for You today with *J-O-Y.*

ANSWER CHECK:

Real heroes...
find joy in helping others.

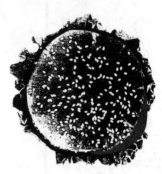

Giant on the Inside

I know a guy who is probably only four feet tall, but inside he's a real giant. Zane Mills has a problem with his nervous system that makes even ordinary things like brushing teeth and turning off the TV big and difficult. He can't walk and sometimes has a hard time just breathing, but he doesn't let that slow him down.

But Zane decided a long time ago that he would try as hard as he could to do everything well. Even though he couldn't finish his college work to become a doctor like he first wanted, he became a high school teacher in science and math. And he learned to drive a specially equipped car so he could get around by himself.

Everyone knows Zane as a loving, caring person. People hardly notice his small frame because his life shows that he's a giant on the inside—where it really counts.

HERO PRACTICE:

You might feel a lot like Zane Mills when you think you're not tall enough or old enough or good enough at doing something. Take a minute to name the things you *can* do. What are you good at? When have you felt really good about yourself?

TAKE COURAGE:

"However, Christ has given each of us special abilities—whatever he wants us to have out of his rich storehouse of gifts." Ephesians 4:7, TLB

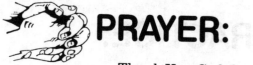 **PRAYER:**

Thank You, God, for me. Thank You for making me just the way I am. Thank You for loving me just the way I am.

ANSWER CHECK: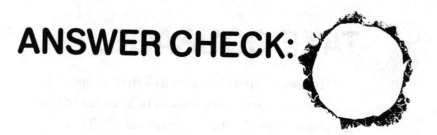

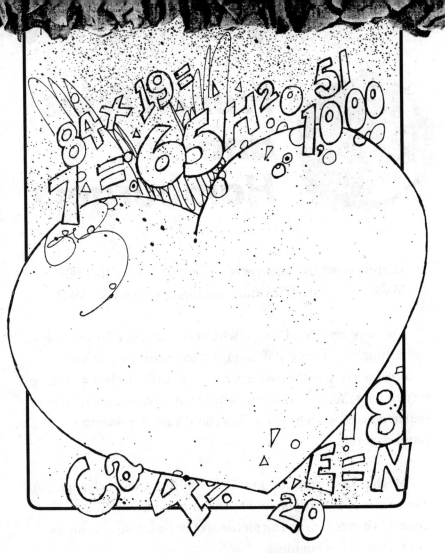

Real heroes...
are learning to use the special gifts God gives them.

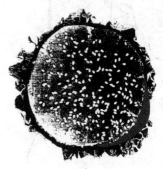

French Fries and Hamburgers

Could you draw a picture of a horse with your toes? Or could you eat french fries and hamburgers with your feet?

One day my friend Anna, who's nine, and her father took me to lunch at Wendy's. When I started eating my baked potato, I noticed some toes reaching up to the table, picking up french fries. You see, Anna was born without arms, so she has learned to eat with her feet. You should see her devour a hamburger!

With a lot of practice (and God's help) Anna has learned to use her feet the way you and I use our hands. One of her favorite things is drawing pictures of horses. She also helps her father in his business.

"Anna is my catalog maker," her father told me. With her feet she arranges the loose pages in order before they are stapled. For Anna, difficulties are just challenges she meets every day.

HERO PRACTICE:

What is the toughest thing you have to do this week? Take a minute to think of what that might be. Remember you can do it with God's help.

TAKE COURAGE:

"I can do everything through him who gives me strength." Philippians 4:13

 **PRAYER:**

I know that You are with me this week, God. One thing I need help with is:

ANSWER CHECK:

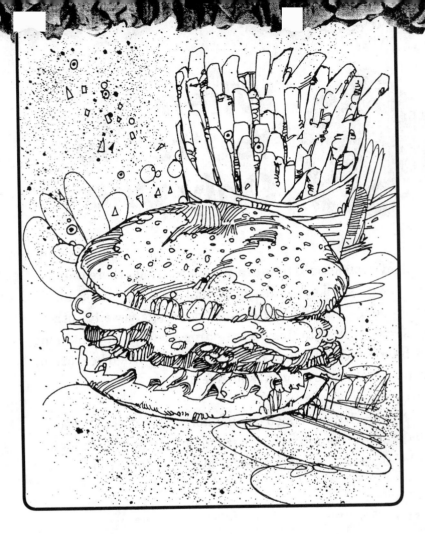

Real heroes . . .
can do anything they need to do with God's help.

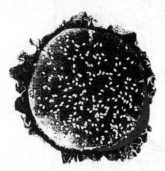

When You're the Only One

Have you noticed that in almost every class there is one kid who gets picked on? In a class that my son Josh was in, everyone teased a girl who couldn't do things as well as other kids could—like running and catching a ball. Josh went along with the mean teasing at first, until one day when he started thinking about how the girl must feel.

Now Josh has stopped teasing her, and that's one reason he's a hero. It takes courage to stand up for what you know is right, especially when you're the only one who will.

HERO PRACTICE:

Next time you're tempted to tease someone in a mean way, remember how you felt when it happened to you. Ask God to help you act kindly, even if you are the only one who does.

TAKE COURAGE:

"Be kind and compassionate to one another."

Ephesians 4:32

 **PRAYER:**

Help me remember, God, how mean teasing feels when I am tempted to do it this week.

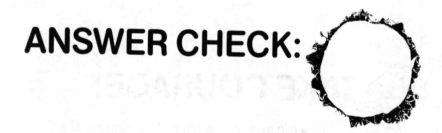

ANSWER CHECK:

Real heroes. . .

stand up for what they know is right, even when they're the only ones who do.

53

Good Morning, God

Don McClean is a great fisherman. Sometimes I think he could catch his limit in a bathtub!

We went backpacking together in the Sierras one summer. When I heard him up making coffee early in the morning, I just rolled over and tried to go back to sleep. But Don was over there roaring with laughter, trying to think up ways to get me out of my sleeping bag. "I'm going to throw you in the river if you don't get out of bed," he laughed.

Groaning, I rolled out. I thought he wanted to go fishing. But Don wanted me to get up and join him for a "good morning" time with God. He believes God is the most important person in his life, and he wants to talk to God and listen to Him first every morning.

Later we did go fishing. As usual, Don caught his limit and I caught two skinny ones.

HERO PRACTICE:

Sometimes it's hard to talk to someone you can't see or hear. That's why it's important to try to make a special time each day when you can get quiet and talk to God. When is the best time in your day for you to talk to God? Where? How can you hear God talk to you?

TAKE COURAGE:

"Be still, and know that I am God." Psalm 46:10

PRAYER:

I need to talk to You, God. And I need to hear what You have to say to me. Thank You for the Bible and for speaking to me through Your words there.

ANSWER CHECK:

Real heroes...
take time to get quiet and talk to God.

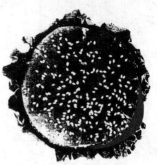

One Small Step

I was in the Los Angeles airport with my sons, Josh and Zac, when I spotted Bob Wieland in a crowd of travelers. "C'mon guys," I said, "this is someone you have to meet."

It's not every day that you get to meet someone who has walked across America. And Bob Wieland did it on his hands! Bob was a six-foot, 205-pound, medical corpsman in Viet Nam when he stepped on a hidden bomb that blew off both his legs. When Bob recovered from the accident he began training, lifting weights to strengthen his body. At first he could only lift five pounds. Today he can lift over 500 pounds in the bench press! It took him 4.9 million "steps" to walk across America, swinging his body along on his hands, wearing thickly padded gloves. He started at Knotts Berry Farm in California on September 8, 1982, and ended up at the Viet Nam War Memorial in Washington D.C. three years, eight months, and six days later! Why did he do it? "To encourage those with legs to take the first step in faith to please God."

Bob knows that when you do that, you are a hero no matter what happens.

HERO PRACTICE:

Bob Wieland started out small when he began lifting weights—only five pounds. You can begin living to please God by doing a very small thing. Where could you start? What could be your "first step"?

TAKE COURAGE:

"Whoever can be trusted with very little can also be trusted with much." Luke 16:10

PRAYER:

I want to please You, God. One small way I can try to please You is:

ANSWER CHECK:

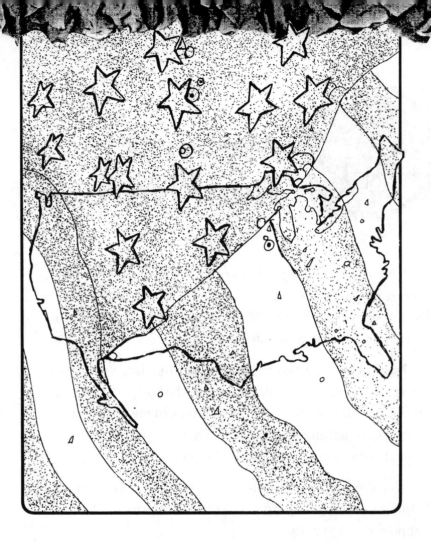

Real heroes . . .
want to please God even in small ways.

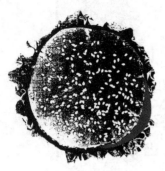

My First Real Hero

It was one of those perfect spring days. My older brother, Steve, and I were playing baseball with some kids up at Volunteer Park. As usual, Steve let me tag along with him and his friends. He was that kind of guy.

I was pitching when one of the kids hit a line drive in my direction. I held out my glove to catch the ball, but instead it hit me right between the eyes and knocked me unconscious. As my fuzzy, aching head cleared, I heard a man running across the field hollering, "Can I help you?"

And then my brother was there, stooping in the dirt, helping me up and saying, "No, I can take care of it. This happens every spring."

It was true. I was always cracking my head open or something, and Steve was always there to help. I guess he was my first real hero—the kind of brother everyone wishes they had, cheering for me, encouraging me, and putting up with me no matter what I did. I can still remember what he always said to me, "Way to go, Bro!"

HERO PRACTICE:

Do you have a brother or sister? How could you be a "hero" to him or her? If you don't have a brother or sister, whom do you know who needs one? Could you volunteer?

TAKE COURAGE:

"Therefore encourage one another and build each other up, just as in fact you are doing."

I Thessalonians 5:11

PRAYER:

Thank You, God, for brothers and sisters, and for some friends who are like brothers or sisters to me. Help me be a hero to them in some way.

ANSWER CHECK:

Real heroes . . .
are learning to be a real "brother" or "sister."

That's Not Fair!

If you stop and listen to kids on the playground or in your backyard, you might hear the words, "That's not fair!"

Bob Wieland had as much right as anyone to use those words when he stepped on a land mine and his legs were blown off in Viet Nam. He had been a good athlete and could have gone back to a promising career in professional baseball. When the medics picked him up from the battle area, he was so badly hurt that they tagged him DOA (dead on arrival). But they didn't count on Bob's courage and faith in God. He surprised everyone by living and leaving the hospital in record time. Never once did he way, "That's not fair! I was a good athlete. I needed my legs." Rather, he said, "God knows what He is doing, and He had a better plan for my life."

Bob was right. Through his efforts he has raised more than $300,000 for needy people and gotten a lot of people thinking about God. Wherever he goes, he encourages people. He says, "Through faith in God, determination, and dedication, there is nothing within the will of God a person can't achieve."

HERO PRACTICE:

Right now you can probably think of at least two things that aren't fair. How can you turn those unfair things around like Bob Wieland did? How could God change those unfair things into something good?

TAKE COURAGE:

"And we know that in all things God works for the good of those who love him, who have been called according to his purpose." Romans 8:28

PRAYER:

It makes me feel a lot better, God, to know that You are here with me. Please help me to see how You can change the unfair things into something good.

ANSWER CHECK:

Real heroes...
trust God to take care of them when things aren't fair.

A Day to Say, "Thank You"

Because of only two minutes without oxygen when she was born, Pam Dahl will spend her life in a wheelchair. She will never walk, and she is unable to do many of the everyday tasks we take for granted.

That's why it's so amazing to learn that Pam has graduated from college and is now working on her master's degree.

Most surprising of all is that Pam *never* complains. She has what I would call a "grateful heart." She is so thankful that God loves her. That's how she keeps that beautiful smile on her face. And that's why she is one of my heroes.

HERO PRACTICE:

You can probably think of many things to complain about every day—parents always reminding you of chores, brothers and sisters who won't leave you alone. Maybe it's your hair, too curly or sticks up where it shouldn't. Just for one day try saying "thank you" instead of complaining, and see how you feel by the end of the day.

TAKE COURAGE:

"Give thanks in all circumstances, for this is God's will for you in Christ Jesus."

I Thessalonians 5:18

71

PRAYER:

Lord, I have a lot to be thank for. Here are some of the things I'm thinking about right now:

ANSWER CHECK:

Real heroes . . .
remember to tell God "Thank You."

The Strongest Man in the World

When I was in grade school I thought being a Christian was just for "sissies." If you were a Christian, you were probably a weak person.

In college, I went to a meeting with a bunch of other football and rugby players like myself and met Paul Anderson. He weighed 300 pounds and was all muscle. During the meeting, he had about twenty of us guys come up front and get on a table. Then he got under it and lifted us all up! He then stood up, looked at the group and said quietly, "I'm the strongest man in the world." (He really is. He holds the world's record for lifting the most weight, which is 6,270 pounds!) "But," he said, "I couldn't make it through a day without the power of Jesus Christ. If I'm not embarrassed to say that, I don't know why any of you should be."

Paul is one of my heroes because he wasn't ashamed to be a Christian, and because he helped me decide to give my life to Jesus Christ.

HERO PRACTICE:

It takes courage to be a Christian and stand up for what you know is right. If you've been ashamed to be known as a Christian as I was, ask God for courage today.

TAKE COURAGE:

"I am not ashamed of the gospel, because it is the power of God for the salvation of everyone who believes." Romans 1:16

 **PRAYER:**

Thank You for courage, Lord. I need courage to be a Christian. Help me not to be ashamed to stand up for what is right.

ANSWER CHECK:

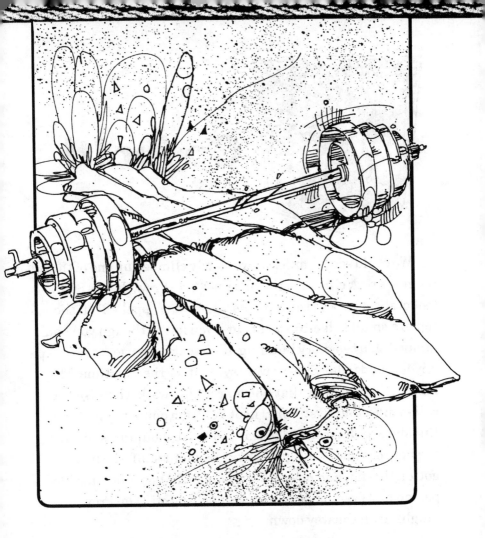

Real heroes . . .
are not ashamed of being known as a Christian.

Go for It!

We could see for miles as we slowly climbed up one of the toughest rock climbs in the Sierras–"The Prow." It was 800 feet of sheer rock to the top. And when you rappelled[1] off the top to a small ledge 150 feet below, you felt as though you had jumped off a ten-story building. It's a scary experience for anyone, and today Sherry was trying it for the first time. The incredible thing was that Sherry couldn't walk. Her disease, called muscular dystrophy,[2] kept her from doing many things. But she was determined to learn to climb mountains. With the help of some of the guys on the Summit staff, she had gotten this far, and now she was doing what no other disabled person had ever done–she was rappelling off "The Prow," laughing all the way down.

This was no surprise to any of us. Sherry had found in God the courage to love herself as she is and live life as fully as possible. That's why when she heard about our GO FOR IT mountain climbing program for the disabled, she said, "I'm gonna go."

HERO PRACTICE:

All of us have certain characteristics that we see as "handicaps"–a nose that's too big, clumsy feet, shy personality, etc. What is your handicap? Remember, God can help you love yourself just the way you are.

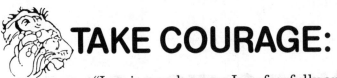

TAKE COURAGE:

"I praise you because I am fearfully and wonderfully made; your works are wonderful, I know that full well." Psalm 139:14

---

[1] Rappel: to lower yourself down a cliff by ropes that are attached to your harness and to the top of the cliff.
[2] Muscular dystrophy: a hereditary disease characterized by gradual weakening of muscles.

PRAYER:

Dear God, there are certain things about myself that I wish were different. Help me to learn to love even that part of me the way You do.

ANSWER CHECK:

Real heroes...
**are learning to
like themselves
as they are.**

A Real Friend

I don't know about you, but sometimes when I'm with someone who can do things a lot better than I can, I feel yucky about myself. That's why my friend Jack Meyer is a real hero to me.

Jack is just the right weight and he's strong. These days I'm kind of overweight and not so strong. Jack is a good athlete. Before I had a mountain-climbing accident it was easy for me to be a good athlete, too. Now it's very hard.

But when Jack and I go to a gym to work out together, he won't let me feel bad about myself. He just encourages me the whole time we're there. He makes me believe that I can do anything if I try. He's a real friend.

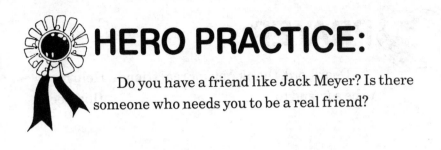

HERO PRACTICE:

Do you have a friend like Jack Meyer? Is there someone who needs you to be a real friend?

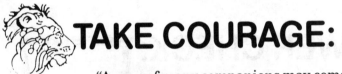

TAKE COURAGE:

"A man of many companions may come to ruin, but there is a friend who sticks closer than a brother." Proverbs 18:24

 **PRAYER:**

Dear Lord, thank You for real friends. Help me to be a friend to _____ this week.

ANSWER CHECK:

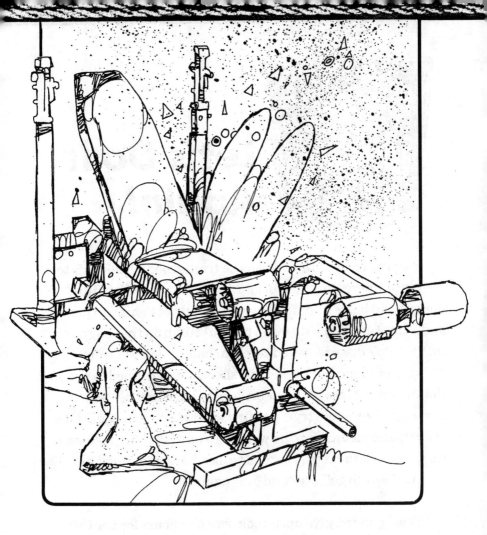

Real heroes . . .
see the best in others.

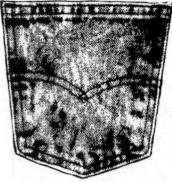

Let's Do It Again!

We pushed Pam Dahl down the trail in her wheelchair to the place where the climb began. Then Amy and Kay lifted her out and helped her to the ground. Jill got behind to push, and Pam started her slow and painful climb up the rough rocks. Pam's disease, called cerebral palsy,[1] kept her from walking or using her hands, but she was determined to get up that mountain. So, with her arms bent back and her feet working like motors trying to find a foothold, she wiggled her body up the mountain. She worked so hard that her face was right against the rock. I turned to look back and heard her saying, "Way to go!" over and over again.

Pam wouldn't give up. It took over two hours for her to reach the top, with Amy, Kay, and Jill helping all the way. So I couldn't believe what she said as she lifted her scratched face and grinned at us. "Let's do it again!"

HERO PRACTICE:

When I remember how Pam wouldn't give up, it makes me try harder to keep going when I want to quit. Think of something you have to do that makes you feel like quitting.

TAKE COURAGE:

"Be strong and courageous . . . Do not be afraid or discouraged, for the Lord God, my God, is with you."

I Chronicles 28:20

---

[1] Cerebral palsy: a disability that affects muscle coordination.

PRAYER:

It's hard to keep going when I feel like quitting, Lord. Thank You for being there to help.

ANSWER CHECK:

Real heroes . . .
never stop trying.

A Teacher You Can Count On

Kids at Whittier Christian High School in California are getting used to seeing a little man in a large, shiny wheelchair zip through the halls on his way to class. Zane Mills is the math and science teacher—the one with the great sense of humor and the one that kids know they can count on. He listens to them. They know that Zane really cares, and he'll do anything he can to encourage them.

Zane is a hero. His disability makes it so hard for him to do even the simplest things that nobody would blame him if he just used his energy on himself all day. But Zane loves the Lord, and he has decided that living for God means really loving people. That's what he does.

HERO PRACTICE:

It's easy to forget that being a Christian means loving other people. What loving things could you do for your family this week?... For your friends?

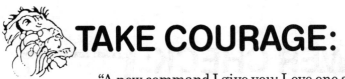

TAKE COURAGE:

"A new command I give you: Love one another. As I have loved you, so you must love one another."

John 13:34

PRAYER:

I know at least one person, Lord, who needs to be loved. Help me think of what I can do to love that person.

ANSWER CHECK:

Real heroes...
show their love
for others.

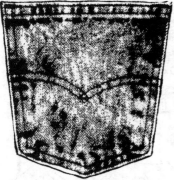

Old Chevy or New Corvette?

If you had your choice between a new Corvette and a beat-up old Chevy, you'd probably be like most people. You'd choose the Corvette. Or, what if you could choose to make either $100,000 or $15,000 a year? What would you choose? Well, that's not hard. You would choose $100,000, of course. Then why would someone choose the old beat-up car and less money if they didn't have to? That's what makes Craig Schindler a hero.

I met Craig in college. He was one of the most brilliant students there, and one of the most popular. He was always staying up half the night listening to someone's problems. Craig went on to become a university professor, a lawyer, and a psychologist. But Craig was very concerned about what might happen to kids like you if someone didn't start talking about big issues like preventing nuclear war and saving our environment. So he organized a group called "Project Victory" that gets important people together to talk seriously about the future. He doesn't make much money and he drives a beat-up old car, but Craig is happiest doing what he knows is the most important job for him.

HERO PRACTICE:

Right now, you probably don't think much about the future—when you will be grown up. God wants to prepare you to make good choices as a grown-up. Ask Him to help you get ready now for the future He has planned for you.

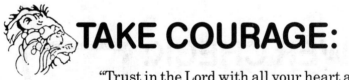

TAKE COURAGE:

"Trust in the Lord with all your heart and lean not on your own understanding; in all your ways acknowledge him, and he will make your paths straight." Proverbs 3:5, 6

 **PRAYER:**

The future seems a long way off, Lord, but help me get ready for it now. Help me to make good choices.

ANSWER CHECK:

Real heroes . . .
know what's really important in life.

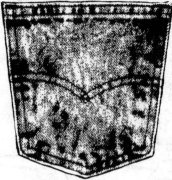

I'll Go Anywhere, Except . . .

Mike Edwards is a modern-day Jonah. He grew up as a farm kid who didn't know anything about the city. In college, when he got serious about being a Christian, he said, "God, You can do anything with my life, except I don't want to go into the inner city, and I don't want to work with poor people."

What Mike couldn't see is that God knows each of us far better than we know ourselves. He knew that Mike would actually love working in the inner city with poor people, if he ever had an opportunity to try it. So God arranged a way for Mike to try it.

Today, Mike works in a rescue mission on skid row in Los Angeles, giving food and clothing to the homeless, and teaching them the Bible. And there's no place else he'd rather be.

HERO PRACTICE:

Like Mike, you and I sometimes pray, "God, I'll do anything... except." How can this prayer change when we remember that God loves us and knows exactly what will make us happy?

TAKE COURAGE:

"The steps of good men are directed by the Lord. He delights in each step they take."

Psalms 37:23, TLB

 **PRAYER:**

Dear God, thank You for knowing better than I do exactly what will make me happy. Help me to trust You.

ANSWER CHECK:

Real heroes...
trust God with their future.

Pedaling in Hawaii

Imagine yourself pedaling your bike down the road in Hawaii. Sound great? Now imagine yourself pedaling 112 miles through blackened lava fields under a scorching sun with vicious winds doing their best to blow you the other way. And imagine that before the bike ride, you had just finished a two-mile swim in the ocean, and when you get off your bike, you'll still have to run twenty-six miles!

That's what you'd have to do if you entered the famous Iron Man Triathlon in Hawaii. And that's what Dr. Ken Campbell did a few years after his body was badly burned in a car crash.

Why did he do something that hard? Because Ken has learned that he feels the best about himself when he decides to do something hard (when he sets a goal) and then does it (finishes the goal). He feels better about the burn scars on his body when he asks his body to do difficult things, and then works hard until his body does them. It all fits in with his greatest goal of all—to live for Jesus Christ every day of his life.

HERO PRACTICE:

What difficult thing could you choose to work on until it's finished? Maybe it's finishing your homework every day this week, or going out for the soccer team and not quitting in the middle of the season. Or maybe you'd like to try racing (start with one or two kilometer races) like Dr. Ken does.

TAKE COURAGE:

"I have fought the good fight, I have finished the race, I have kept the faith." II Timothy 4:7

PRAYER:

Dear God, I don't want to be a quitter. Help me to set goals and keep working on them even when I don't feel like it.

ANSWER CHECK:

Real heroes. . .
set clear goals and go after them.

Joni

Joni was a pretty, happy, active teenager who loved the Lord when she broke her neck in a diving accident. After she was pulled out of the water, she realized that she couldn't feel anything from her neck down. Since that time, Joni's legs and arms have been paralyzed. But instead of feeling sorry for herself, Joni got busy. She learned how to operate a motorized wheelchair. She learned how to feed herself, using her neck muscles and special arm straps. She learned how to drive a specially equipped van. And she even learned how to paint beautiful pictures, holding the brush with her teeth.

I met Joni about four years ago when we talked together about our GO FOR IT program for the physically disabled. I was amazed to hear about the many ways she was helping other disabled people. Joni has learned that a real hero takes the worst that can happen and lets the Lord turn it into something good.

HERO PRACTICE:

What is the worst thing that has happened to you this year? How could God turn this into something good?

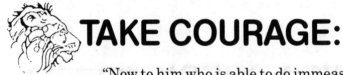

TAKE COURAGE:

"Now to him who is able to do immeasurably more than all we ask or imagine, according to his power that is at work within us. . ." Ephesians 3:20

 **PRAYER:**

My worst thing isn't as bad as Joni's, Lord. But sometimes it feels as bad. Thank You that You can turn my worst thing into something good, just as You did for Joni.

ANSWER CHECK:

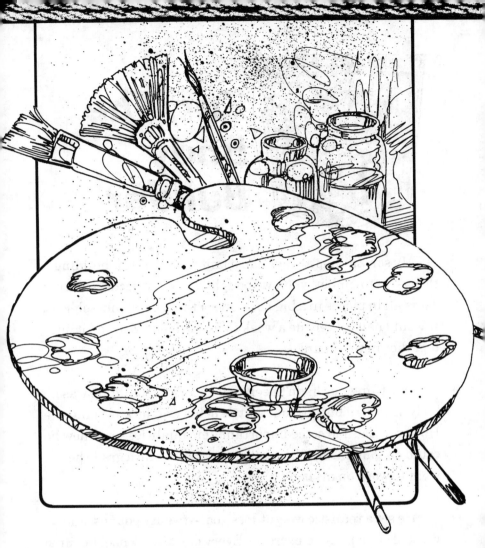

Real heroes...
trust God no matter what happens.

Zac, The Body Builder

My son Zac has always had a fantastic mind for building things. I remember when we bought a new barbecue grill that came all in pieces in a big box—one of those do-it-yourself jobs. It would have taken me a week to figure it out. Zac had it put together in two hours.

One thing Zac hadn't been real successful building was his body. He was a big guy, but a little of his weight wasn't muscle. However, Zac had some important hero qualities—he knew he could do something if he really tried. So, in ninth grade he went to work on his body.

He set a realistic weight-loss goal—twenty pounds, and worked out a plan for exercise. Every day after school he lifted weights and played racquetball at a local gym. In less than six weeks, Zac had reached his goal, and is now setting new goals. It was hard, especially when his brother, who never gains weight, was eating all the "good" stuff Zac loves. But he stayed with the program and now he feels better about himself than ever before.

HERO PRACTICE:

Most of us have trouble sticking with something, especially when it takes a long time. For you it might be piano lessons, or a science project, or even losing weight, like Zac. Remember that God is interested in everything you do, and will help you stick with it.

TAKE COURAGE:

"The Christ you have to deal with is not a weak person outside you, but a tremendous power inside you." II Corinthians 13:3, Phillips

PRAYER:

I'm thankful, God, that You care about me so much that You will help me with:

ANSWER CHECK:

Real heroes...
count on God to help them reach their goals.

Oh, Silly Me!

Maybe you're like me. Sometimes I don't even try to do certain things because I'm afraid I'll make a mistake. Then I think of Mark—one of my heroes.

Mark was born without hands. I suppose he could have decided to stay in the house all his life so no one could make fun of him when he made mistakes. Instead, Mark learned to do many things—write, throw a football, play a trombone, play tennis—with the stubs on the ends of his arms. He even went to college where he was an All-American football player, and then became a high school coach.

Sometimes Mark makes mistakes, but he always tries to do his best. And if he messes up, he gets a funny grin on his face and says, "Oh, silly me." Then he tries again.

HERO PRACTICE:

Everybody makes mistakes. It's the people who refuse to let mistakes keep them from trying again who are the real heroes.

TAKE COURAGE:

"In God I trust; I will not be afraid."

Psalm 56:4b

PRAYER:

Dear God, I know You will help me be the best I can be. One thing I need courage for is _____.

Thank You that I don't have to be afraid of making mistakes.

ANSWER CHECK:

Real heroes . . .
don't get discouraged by their mistakes.

Hey, Champ, You Can Do It!

Have you ever heard a kid say, "Hey, stupid. I'll bet your mother dropped you on your head." Sometimes kids (and adults, too) put people down who aren't good at things like sports or math, or they make fun of people who don't dress right.

One of my heroes is Coach Parks. He knows that God made every kid special, and that's how Coach treats everybody. When we were coaching high school sports together, a kid named Henry came out who was not very athletic. He was fifteen, but he looked about ten. And he was usually about forty yards behind everyone else. Coach Parks started running alongside Henry in practice, hollering encouraging words like, "Way to go, Champ!" and "Hey, Champ, you can do it!" Soon Henry began to feel like a real winner, and he ran better than he ever thought he could.

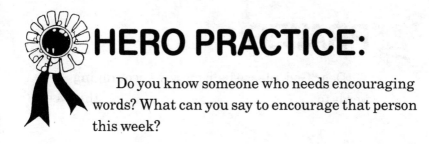

HERO PRACTICE:

Do you know someone who needs encouraging words? What can you say to encourage that person this week?

TAKE COURAGE:

"Therefore encourage one another and build each other up." I Thessalonians 5:11

PRAYER:

Dear God, please help me say encouraging
words to _____ this week.

ANSWER CHECK:

Real heroes...
encourage other people.

Do you know any *real heroes*? In what ways have you been a real hero since reading this book? When is it most difficult for you to be a real hero?

Tim Hansel would like to hear your answers to these questions. You can write to him at:

Tim Hansel
c/o Chariot Books
850 N. Grove Ave.
Elgin, IL 60120

For more mystery and adventure, read
Mystery on Mirror Mountain

Can Johnny let God "stand up tall and strong inside him?"

Johnny Finlay thought living on Mirror Mountain was the greatest thing that could happen to a kid. But then the judge said he had to go back down the mountain to school. Three years was a long time to be away from school . . . and friends. Everything seemed harder—especially making new friends. He didn't fit in.

Johnny yearned to stay on the mountain and help his Great Aunt Lou with her wild herb business. But whether he's on the mountain or in school, Johnny struggles to "let God stand up tall and strong inside him," because as Aunt Lou reminds him, "The Lord don't come into nobody just to set down and twiddle His thumbs."

You'll find this and other Mirror Mountain books by WYNNETTE FRASER at your local Christian bookstore:

Mystery on   ISBN 1-55513-588-9
  Mirror Mountain

Courage on   ISBN 1-55513-039-9
  Mirror Mountain

Mystery at   ISBN 1-55513-717-2
  Deepwood Bay

❧ PARENTS ❧

Are you looking for fun ways to bring the Bible to life in the lives of your children?

Chariot Family Publishing has hundreds of books, toys, games, and videos that help teach your children the Bible and apply it to their everyday lives.

Look for these educational, inspirational, and fun products at your local Christian bookstore.